PRAYERSCRIPTS

Speaking God's Word Book Edition

DESTROY THE ENEMY

30 Days of Prayers for

BREAKING STRONGHOLDS AND CANCELLING EVIL WORKS BY GOD'S AUTHORITY

CYRIL OPOKU

Destroy the Enemy: *Breaking Strongholds and Cancelling Evil Works by God's Authority*

Published by *Quest Publications*

ISBN: 978-1-988439-78-5

Cover design by *Quest Publications (questpublications@outlook.com)*

Unless otherwise indicated, all Scripture quotations are taken from the World English Bible WEB, which is in the public domain. For more information, visit: www.worldenglish.bible

This book is a work of devotional encouragement. It is not intended to replace biblical study, pastoral counsel, or professional therapy.

Printed in the United States of America.

First Edition: August 2025

For more books like this, visit *PrayerScripts:* https://prayerscripts.org

CONTENTS

PREFACE

"For the weapons of our warfare are not of the flesh, but mighty before God to the throwing down of strongholds."
—2 Corinthians 10:4 WEB

We live in a world where unseen battles rage every day. These battles are not merely physical, nor are they confined to what the natural eye can see. Behind the cycles of oppression, sudden losses, inexplicable resistance, and relentless attacks lies a spiritual enemy who seeks to steal, kill, and destroy. Many believers love God, yet they find themselves entangled in hidden snares, weighed down by generational strongholds, or assaulted by relentless evil works. This is why this book was written.

Destroy the Enemy: Breaking Strongholds and Cancelling Evil Works by God's Authority is more than a collection of prayers; it is a weapon in your hand. It is designed to awaken you to the authority you already possess in Christ. Through Scripture and prophetic prayer, you will be equipped to confront the adversary without fear, to tear down entrenched works of darkness, and to establish God's dominion over your life and family.

Too many of God's people live beneath their inheritance because they have not learned to wage war with the authority given them through the blood of Jesus and the Word of God. It is not enough to simply recognize the presence of the enemy; we must rise up in faith and command his works to be destroyed.

Each prayer in these pages is Spirit-led, rooted in the unshakable Word of God, and tailored to help you declare victory in every area of your life. As you walk through these Scriptures and prayers, you will not only break the grip of the enemy but also step into the freedom, peace, and power that Christ secured for you on the cross.

May this book stir holy boldness within you. May it teach your hands to war and your fingers to fight. And may every stronghold be shattered as you take your stand in the authority of God.

Ready at His command,
Cyril O. *(Illinois, August 2025)*

Introduction

The enemy is real—and so is your authority to defeat him.

Every day, whether we recognize it or not, we are engaged in a spiritual conflict. Evil forces work tirelessly to plant fear, sickness, strife, confusion, and bondage into the lives of God's people. The strategies may look different—generational strongholds, sudden setbacks, unseen resistance, or relentless oppression—but the agenda is the same: to weaken your faith and steal the blessings secured for you in Christ.

This book, *Destroy the Enemy: Breaking Strongholds and Cancelling Evil Works by God's Authority*, is a spiritual arsenal for those who refuse to be passive in the face of warfare. It is a collection of prophetic, Scripture-rooted prayers crafted to equip you to stand boldly against the works of darkness. Here you will not find empty words or powerless formulas, but declarations grounded in the living Word of God—designed to expose, confront, and overthrow the enemy's operations in your life and household.

Each prayer aligns with a specific Scripture, unfolding the truth of God's promises while teaching you how to wield them effectively in battle. You will learn what it means to root out, pull down, and utterly destroy every demonic work standing in opposition to God's plan for you. At the same time, these prayers establish God's peace, protection, and blessing, ensuring that once the strongholds are torn down, His Kingdom is firmly planted in their place.

This book is a practical, Spirit-filled guide to spiritual warfare, giving you prayers to cancel evil works, dismantle hidden strongholds, and enforce the victory Christ has already won for you. Here, you will discover not just how to pray, but how to pray with authority—so that your words carry the weight of Heaven against the forces of Hell.

HOW TO USE THIS BOOK

This is not a book to be rushed through. Each of the 30 prayers is structured as a daily prayer journey, combining the Word of God with prophetic, Spirit-led intercession. Here's how you can make the most of it:

1. **Start with the Scripture** – Each prayer begins with a verse from the World English Bible (WEB). Read it slowly and aloud, letting the Word sink into your heart.

2. **Declare the Word** – Meditate on the key truth in the verse, affirming it as God's unchanging promise.

3. **Pray with Authority** – Use the written prayer as a guide. Speak it boldly, personally, and with conviction. Replace "I" with your name or the names of loved ones as needed.

4. **Journal Insights** – Keep a notebook nearby. Write down any impressions, warnings, or directions you sense from the Holy Spirit.

5. **Build a Rhythm** – Pray one Scripture each day, or linger longer on those that strike you deeply. Repetition builds sharpness, and sharpness builds victory.

Whether you walk through these prayers privately in your devotional time, with your family, or in a small group, the key is consistency. Each prayer is a sword in your hand—use it faithfully.

DAY 1

THE WORKS OF SATAN BROKEN

"He who sins is of the devil, for the devil has been sinning from the beginning. To this end the Son of God was revealed: that he might destroy the works of the devil."
— 1 John 3:8 WEB

Lord of Hosts, I stand in awe of the revelation that the Son of God was manifested to destroy the works of the devil. I declare with holy fire that every work of darkness targeted against me, my family, and my destiny is shattered by the authority of Jesus Christ. Sin is broken, curses are overturned, and every demonic plan is reduced to ashes.

Father, I expose and renounce the works of the enemy in every area of my life. Where he has sown lies, let Your truth uproot them. Where he has plotted destruction, let Your hand of power demolish it. Where he has built strongholds, let the fire of Your Spirit tear them down brick by brick. I declare destruction upon fear, destruction upon sickness, destruction upon oppression, and destruction upon every yoke that seeks to bind me.

I thank You, Lord, that Jesus did not come to negotiate with darkness but to utterly destroy it. Therefore, I will not tolerate compromise, I will not allow hidden sin, and I will not leave open doors for the enemy to exploit. I align myself with Christ's mission to see the devil's works exposed and broken forever.

Today I decree that my household is free from every plot of the evil one. The works of witchcraft, manipulation, and rebellion crumble in the presence of the Son of God. We walk in liberty, truth, and victory, for the destroyer of the devil's works lives in us. In Jesus' name, Amen.

DAY 2

Breaking Every Stronghold

For the weapons of our warfare are not of the flesh, but mighty before God to the throwing down of strongholds, throwing down imaginations and every high thing that is exalted against the knowledge of God, and bringing every thought into captivity to the obedience of Christ.
— 2 Corinthians 10:4-5 WEB

Almighty God, I lift my voice in battle cry today. You have armed me not with earthly weapons but with divine power to tear down strongholds. I declare that no fortress of darkness can withstand the force of Your Spirit working through me. Every high thing that exalts itself against Your truth must bow. Every false argument and rebellious thought must submit to the authority of Christ.

Lord, I come against every stronghold raised over my life and family—fear, addiction, doubt, generational bondage, and every fortress built by lies. By Your power, I pull them down brick by brick until nothing remains but freedom and truth. Every proud obstacle that seeks to resist Your will is demolished.

I decree that the battlefield of my mind is cleansed. Every thought not aligned with Christ is taken captive and brought into obedience. No more will my mind be a playground for the enemy; it is now the dwelling place of the Spirit of God.

Father, establish in my household a fortress of righteousness, faith, and peace. Let the enemy's walls crumble, his plots disintegrate, and his voice be silenced. Where strongholds once stood, let altars of worship arise. Where chains once bound, let liberty flow.

In Jesus' name, Amen.

DAY 3

BREAKING THE THIEF'S AGENDA

"The thief only comes to steal, kill, and destroy. I came that
they may have life, and may have it abundantly."
—John 10:10 WEB

O Lord of Glory, my Shield and my Defender, I rise in holy defiance
against the agenda of the thief. I declare that the works of the
destroyer against me and my family are broken. Every attempt to
rob us of peace, provision, or purpose is exposed and annihilated
by the power of Christ.

Father, I cancel the enemy's mission to sow destruction in my
household. His schemes to kill dreams, destroy relationships, and
steal blessings are nullified by the Word of God and the Blood of
Jesus. I decree that no power of darkness will succeed in limiting
my destiny or that of my family.

Lord Jesus, You came to give abundant life. I proclaim that life over
every area the enemy has targeted for death. Where the adversary
sought to destroy, I declare restoration. Where he tried to steal, I
command a sevenfold return. Where he planned death, I release
resurrection power.

Almighty God, let every demonic altar raised against my life
crumble into ashes. Let every generational curse, every word of
destruction, and every hidden plot be shattered by Your mighty
hand. I stand in the finished work of Christ, declaring the enemy's
agenda destroyed. In Jesus' name, Amen.

DAY 4

THE GATES WILL NOT PREVAIL

I also tell you that you are Peter, and on this rock I will build my assembly, and the gates of Hades will not prevail against it.
— Matthew 16:18 WEB

Rock of Ages, I stand in the power of Your unshakable promise. You are building Your church, and I am part of that victorious assembly. No gate of hell, no demonic fortress, no entrenched stronghold can withstand the advancing power of Christ's kingdom.

Father, in the name of Jesus, I speak destruction over every structure of darkness erected against me and my family. Let the foundations of wickedness crumble. Let the walls of opposition fall. Let every demonic barricade collapse under the weight of Christ's authority. Hell cannot prevail where the Rock stands firm.

I cancel the assignments of the enemy designed to frustrate destiny, delay breakthroughs, or silence our voices. Strongholds of generational bondage, be torn down. Altars of witchcraft and manipulation, be consumed by fire. Every gate standing against our progress is destroyed, because the gates of Hades cannot resist the march of God's people.

Lord, I thank You for making us unshakable in Christ. We will not retreat, we will not bow, we will not fear. The church is rising in victory, and my family is secured in that triumph. The power of darkness is destroyed forever. In Jesus' name, Amen.

DAY 5

END OF THE ENEMY

"The devil who deceived them was thrown into the lake of fire and sulfur, where the beast and the false prophet are also. They will be tormented day and night forever and ever."
— Revelation 20:10 WEB

Righteous Judge of all the earth, I exalt You for Your justice and Your everlasting dominion. The destiny of the enemy is sealed, his defeat eternal, his torment unending. I rejoice in the assurance that Satan and every worker of iniquity aligned with him are condemned to destruction, unable to overturn Your decree.

Lord, I invoke this finished verdict over my life and my family. Every stronghold raised against us collapses. Every deceptive structure erected to block our progress is consumed by holy fire. The spirit of destruction that the enemy sends is reversed and returned to its sender. I declare that no plan of darkness will stand, for the Lamb has triumphed and sealed the fate of the dragon.

Father, arise and let every lingering shadow of wickedness be shattered. Let curses be reversed, chains be broken, and cycles of oppression end. The enemy's schemes are exposed, his operations destroyed, his foundation overturned. What he planned for evil is rendered powerless by Your mighty hand.

I decree that my household walks in the reality of this victory. No demonic throne will rule over us, no deceptive power will seduce us, and no force of darkness will prevail. The devil is doomed, and his works are destroyed.

In Jesus' name, Amen.

DAY 6

OVERCOME EVIL WITH GOOD

Don't be overcome by evil, but overcome evil with good.
—Romans 12:21 WEB

Mighty Father, Righteous Judge, and Consuming Fire, I rise in Your presence today declaring that evil will not rule over me or my household. I am not a victim of darkness, for Your light shines within me and through me. Every scheme of the enemy designed to corrupt my heart, poison my mind, or derail my destiny is dismantled by the authority of Your Word. The flood of evil intentions raised against me will be swallowed up in the sea of Your goodness, mercy, and truth.

Lord, I declare that the voice of hatred, bitterness, and vengeance will find no dwelling in me. I overcome malice with mercy. I overcome cursing with blessing. I overcome attacks with the armor of righteousness. Every arrow launched against me in the secret places is returned empty and powerless because I choose the higher ground of Your Spirit.

Let the works of darkness collapse under the weight of divine love and truth. Let every snare laid against me become a testimony of Your faithfulness. In every confrontation with evil, I will not bow to fear or wrath, for I am clothed with Your peace and guided by Your wisdom.

Father, I decree that in my family line, evil cycles are broken, strongholds are shattered, and generational iniquities are destroyed. From this day, goodness will pursue us, and righteousness will shield us. Your glory rises upon us like the sun, scattering the night forever.

In Jesus' name, Amen.

DAY 7

THE STRONGER ONE PREVAILS

But when someone stronger attacks him and overcomes
him, he takes from him his whole armor in which he
trusted, and divides his plunder.
—Luke 11:22 WEB

Lord God Almighty, my Strong Deliverer, I proclaim today that You
are the Stronger One who fights for me and my family. No fortress
of the wicked can withstand Your power, and no armor of the
enemy can shield him from Your hand. Every evil power that
trusted in lies, enchantments, or wicked devices is stripped bare
before You. You are the Lion of Judah, roaring over my life and
scattering those who dared to resist Your dominion.

I decree that every demonic guard stationed against my destiny is
overthrown. Every strong man assigned to monitor, hinder, or
oppress my household is bound and plundered by the fire of the
Holy Spirit. Lord, invade the camp of the enemy and seize back
everything stolen—peace, health, opportunities, wealth, and joy.
What the enemy trusted in is now dissolved under the weight of
Your glory.

O God of justice, arise and dismantle satanic shields erected over
my bloodline. Let every barrier crumble, and let every wall fall flat.
The weapons of darkness cannot prevail when Your light pierces
through. By Your might, I declare total victory and total recovery.

From this day, I walk free, and my family walks free. We step out of captivity into abundance. We rise from the shadows into marvelous light. We march forward clothed in the triumph of Christ, never again to be subdued.

In Jesus' name, Amen.

DAY 8

More Than Conquerors

No, in all these things, we are more than conquerors
through him who loved us.
—Romans 8:37 WEB

Everlasting Father, King of Glory, I lift my voice to declare that I am
not merely surviving the battles of life—I am more than a
conqueror through Christ Jesus. The forces of hell may rage, but
Your love secures my victory. No trial, no demon, no adversary can
strip away the triumph purchased by the blood of the Lamb. I do
not fight for victory; I fight from victory already sealed in Your Son.

I declare that every storm the enemy sends only becomes a platform
for Your glory. Every attack against my household will backfire and
turn into a testimony of deliverance. The conspiracies of the wicked
are frustrated, their counsel overturned, and their efforts scattered
to the wind. In every circumstance, we emerge not bruised victims
but radiant victors, shining with the light of Christ.

Lord, I decree that the power of conquest flows through me daily.
My mind conquers fear. My heart conquers bitterness. My spirit
conquers despair. My family conquers generational chains, for the
covenant of love has spoken louder than curses.

I embrace this reality, Father, that I am never defeated. Even in
battle, I rise. Even in struggle, I shine. Your love sustains me, and
Your Spirit empowers me. The shout of triumph will never leave my
lips, for my destiny is secured in Christ. In Jesus' name, Amen.

DAY 9

THE DAY OF THE WICKED IS COMING

The Lord will laugh at him, for he sees that his day is
coming.
—Psalm 37:13 WEB

O Lord, the Ancient of Days, You sit enthroned above the nations
and laugh at the pride of the wicked. You see the end from the
beginning, and You declare that the days of the enemy are
numbered. Father, I rejoice that no adversary can exalt himself
forever over me or my household, for You have decreed their
downfall.

I decree that every proud enemy who thought my family would
remain in bondage is now exposed to divine judgment. Their
boasting is silenced, and their strongholds are shattered. They
plotted secretly, but You have uncovered them openly. You laugh at
their futile attempts because the day of reckoning hastens like a
storm against their camp.

Lord, I declare that my household will not be mocked or shamed by
the enemy. Instead, the laughter of heaven will fill our mouths as we
see the wicked stumble into their own pits. The works of evil are
dismantled, the curses reversed, and the arrows broken. No
adversary can outlast Your patience or escape Your judgment.

Today, I stand in holy confidence, knowing that You fight for me.
Though the wicked may rage for a moment, their end is certain, and

their defeat is sure. I align myself with Your purposes and rejoice in Your unfailing justice.

In Jesus' name, Amen.

DAY 10

Through God We Triumph

Through God we will do valiantly, for it is he who will
tread down our enemies.
—Psalm 60:12 WEB

Mighty God, Lord of Hosts, I rise in faith to declare that my
strength comes from You alone. I will not rely on human ability, nor
will I trust in the arm of flesh. Through You, I will do valiantly, for
You are the One who crushes the enemy underfoot. Every
adversary that lifted itself against me and my household is subdued
by Your mighty hand.

Father, I decree that my family will not live in fear of wicked powers.
No enemy, whether seen or unseen, can stand before the fire of Your
presence. By Your Spirit, I tread on serpents and scorpions, and
over all the power of the enemy. Every demonic assault launched
against our health, peace, and destiny is crushed and rendered
powerless.

Lord, we will not walk in defeat. We rise in courage, knowing that
the victory is already ours in Christ Jesus. You are our Commander,
and under Your leadership we march forward with boldness. Every
battle becomes a platform for Your glory, and every conflict ends
with songs of triumph.

Through You, Father, we reclaim lost ground, recover stolen
blessings, and establish generational victories. Let the sound of
rejoicing fill our household, for our enemies have been trampled

beneath Your feet. We live in the assurance of Your covenant, walking valiantly with heads lifted high.

In Jesus' name, Amen.

DAY 11

THE LIVING GOD PREVAILS

Yahweh lives! Blessed be my Rock. Exalted be the God of
my salvation!
— Psalm 18:46 WEB

Mighty and Living God, I exalt You as the eternal Rock and the
unshakable foundation of my life. You are not a dead idol, nor a
powerless god. You are alive, active, and victorious. Because You
live, every power of darkness seeking to swallow me and my
household must crumble in defeat. I declare today that You are
exalted above every principality, power, and evil agenda waged
against my destiny.

O God of my salvation, rise and scatter the works of darkness
fashioned against me. Where the enemy has planted strongholds,
let Your consuming fire break them down. Where the wicked have
raised altars to speak against me and my family, let Your living
presence silence them forever. Because You are alive, I will not be
swallowed by the grave; because You reign, my family will not be
buried by shame or destruction.

I call forth the victory of the living God over every assignment of
premature death, sickness, financial ruin, or oppression. Let Your
voice thunder against the strongmen assigned to my lineage. Let
every snare and secret plot be shattered before they manifest. As the
living God, You cannot be defeated, therefore I cannot be defeated.

Father, exalt Yourself in my life. Be lifted high above my enemies. Cause Your light to consume every shadow of death that hovers over my family. Today, I stand anchored in the Rock of Ages, declaring that the Living God reigns, and the wicked works of darkness are no more.

In Jesus' name, Amen.

DAY 12

STRENGTH TO DESTROY STRONGHOLDS

I can do all things through Christ who strengthens me.
— Philippians 4:13 WEB

Lord Jesus Christ, my Strength and my Shield, I stand clothed with Your power and not my own. By Your Spirit, I refuse to bow to fear, defeat, or intimidation from the enemy. I decree today that I can do all things—not in the frailty of my flesh, but through the indestructible strength of Christ within me.

Every assignment of weakness the enemy has projected into my body, my mind, or my spirit is broken now. I rise in divine power to confront the forces of darkness that war against my family. By Christ's strength, I tear down generational strongholds, cancel evil covenants, and overthrow every satanic decree written against my bloodline. What I could not overcome in my own ability, I now overcome by the strength of the Greater One inside me.

O God of might, fortify me with the boldness of a warrior. Let the muscles of my spirit be built in prayer and praise until no demonic attack can shake me. I take strength to confront the unseen battles and prevail against the gates of hell. I will not be weary, for Your strength is made perfect in my weakness.

Today, I decree over my household that no chain will remain unbroken, no curse will remain unshattered, and no altar will remain standing, because Christ is our strength. By His power, we rise victorious and unstoppable. In Jesus' name, Amen.

DAY 13

HEALING BY HOLY FEAR

Don't be wise in your own eyes. Fear Yahweh, and depart
from evil. It will be health to your body, and nourishment
to your bones.
— Proverbs 3:7-8 WEB

Holy and Righteous Father, I humble myself before Your throne. I
renounce the pride of my own wisdom, and I bow in reverence to
You, the Ancient of Days. You are the source of true wisdom, life,
and health. I acknowledge that when I walk in the fear of the Lord
and separate from evil, my body is restored, and my spirit is
renewed.

Today, I declare war against the spirits of arrogance and rebellion
that open the door to sickness, confusion, and destruction. Every
spirit of pride that has sought to infiltrate my family line is uprooted
by fire. I choose to fear the Lord, and in doing so, I cut off the
poisonous roots of evil that drain the strength of my body and the
vitality of my family.

Father, I plead the blood of Jesus over my bones, over my organs,
and over the structure of my household. Let the fear of the Lord
drive out every form of disease and affliction sent as an arrow from
the enemy. Let divine health spring forth, nourishing my flesh and
fortifying my inner man.

By the covenant of Christ's blood, I declare that my family shall not
be plagued with inherited diseases, mental afflictions, or terminal

conditions. We choose the way of the Lord, and therefore, health and wholeness manifest in our lives. I destroy the grip of infirmity, and I command it never to return.

In Jesus' name, Amen.

DAY 14

THE SWORD OF THE SPIRIT

And take the helmet of salvation, and the sword of the
Spirit, which is the word of God.
— Ephesians 6:17 WEB

Lord of Hosts, I lift my voice in triumph, wielding the sharp, two-
edged sword of the Spirit. Your Word in my mouth is not empty
speech, but a weapon of war that cuts through the plans of darkness.
I declare that I am armed with salvation and fortified with divine
authority to destroy the works of the enemy.

O Word of God, go forth like fire and consume every demonic
camp raised against my family. Let every incantation, spell, or curse
sent to derail my destiny be pierced and silenced by the sword of
the Spirit. I refuse to fight in the flesh; I fight with the Word, and
the Word never loses its power.

I decree that every lie of the enemy over my life is dismantled by
truth. Every fiery dart of condemnation, fear, and despair is
extinguished because I wear the helmet of salvation. I stand
untouchable, covered in Christ, and unstoppable in battle. The
Word is my light, my shield, and my victory.

Today, I lift the sword over my children, my family, and my
generations. I sever ties with demonic covenants, I cut down
generational curses, and I destroy hidden works of darkness. As the
Word proceeds from my mouth, I release judgment against every

enemy of my soul. By the sword of the Spirit, I declare total victory. In Jesus' name, Amen.

DAY 15

NO WEAPON SHALL PROSPER

No weapon that is formed against you will prevail; and you will condemn every tongue that rises against you in judgment. This is the heritage of Yahweh's servants, and their righteousness is of me," says Yahweh.
— Isaiah 54:17 WEB

Almighty Defender, I lift my voice in confidence, declaring that every weapon crafted in the forge of hell is shattered before it reaches me. By Your decree, O Lord, no arrow, no spell, no curse, no evil scheme shall prosper against me or my household. You have clothed me in righteousness, and this is my inheritance as Your servant.

Father, I rise in the authority of Your Word to condemn every tongue that speaks against my destiny. I silence accusations, slanders, and judgments spoken in secret places. Every whisper of witchcraft, every pronouncement of failure, every evil decree against my family is canceled and nullified by the blood of Jesus.

I destroy the enemy's works assigned to my lineage. No hidden snare will entrap me, no invisible net will capture my children, and no destructive weapon will strike my family. I take my stand on the covenant of protection that cannot be broken, and I declare that the enemy's efforts are frustrated forever.

This day, O Lord, I walk in the boldness of divine immunity. I trample serpents and scorpions, and nothing shall by any means harm me. Weapons may be formed, but they shall never prosper. Attacks may be launched, but they shall never succeed. For the Lord has spoken, and His Word is final.

In Jesus' name, Amen.

DAY 16

THE ARM OF THE WICKED BROKEN

For the arms of the wicked shall be broken, but Yahweh
upholds the righteous.
— Psalm 37:17 WEB

Mighty Deliverer, I lift my voice in victory today, for You are the
One who upholds me with Your everlasting arms. Every scheme of
the wicked against me and my family is destined to collapse, for the
strength of the enemy cannot withstand Your power. Where they
seek to strike, You have already broken their arm. Where they
attempt to hold us in bondage, their grip is shattered and destroyed.

I decree that every hand stretched out in malice is broken by the fire
of the Lord. Every spiritual oppressor that rises against my
household is struck down. Their weapons are powerless; their
strategies are frustrated. The wicked may conspire, but their
strength has been dissolved by the decree of the Almighty. My
family stands upheld, not by our own might, but by the righteous
right hand of God that never fails.

Lord, I thank You because while the wicked collapse under the
weight of their rebellion, we rise under the covering of Your
righteousness. You sustain our steps, You preserve our lives, and
You cause our light to shine in the midst of darkness. The
stronghold of the wicked is dismantled, and their counsel is
overturned.

Therefore, I stand unafraid, for the power of evil has been broken and its arm severed forever. I live in the assurance that I am carried, preserved, and upheld by the Lord of Hosts. In this confidence, I declare my household untouchable to the schemes of hell.

In Jesus' name, Amen.

DAY 17

THE LAST ENEMY DESTROYED

The last enemy that will be abolished is death.
— 1 Corinthians 15:26 WEB

Eternal Father, I exalt You as the Victor over every enemy. You are the God who conquered the grave and stripped death of its sting. I declare that death and its companions—fear, torment, sickness, and decay—are destroyed in my life and in my family by the triumph of the cross.

By the blood of Jesus, I speak life where the enemy has decreed destruction. Every covenant with premature death is broken, every handwriting of hell erased. I cancel every shadow of the grave that hovers over my destiny, and I decree that my family shall not be swallowed by destruction. For Christ has abolished the final enemy, and His resurrection power flows through me now.

Lord, let Your life-giving Spirit breathe afresh upon my household. Where the enemy plants seeds of despair, let abundant life spring forth. Where death attempts to reign, let Your resurrection glory overrule. My body, my mind, my children, and my generations are sealed in the victory of Jesus' blood.

I declare boldly that no grave can claim us, no sickness can define us, and no power of death can determine our end. We live to fulfill Your purpose, we rise to carry out Your will, and we walk in the assurance that Christ has destroyed death forever. In Jesus' name, Amen.

DAY 18

THE ENEMY FORCED TO FLEE

The foreigners shall fade away, and shall come trembling
out of their close places.
— Psalm 18:45 WEB

Lion of Judah, I lift my shout of triumph, for the enemies that once
harassed me now tremble at the sound of Your name. Every foreign
spirit, every demonic intruder, every unclean power hidden in
secret places is exposed and expelled by Your blazing light.

I decree that no stranger to Your covenant has the right to dwell in
my territory. Every force of darkness that crept into my family, my
health, my finances, or my destiny is commanded to flee in terror.
They cannot remain; they cannot resist the fire of Your presence. By
the authority of Christ, I drive them out, and I establish the
dominion of God over every corner of my life.

O Lord, let the trembling of my enemies be multiplied. Let the fear
of Your majesty cause them to scatter seven ways. I declare my
household to be a habitation of righteousness, where no foreign
spirit can hide. Every hidden enemy in "close places" is uncovered,
uprooted, and banished by the power of the blood.

I stand as an heir of the covenant, claiming my rightful inheritance.
The strangers fade away, and their influence dissolves like smoke
before the wind. My family is free, my path is clear, and the
dominion of Christ is firmly established.

In Jesus' name, Amen.

DAY 19

THE SILENCE OF THE ENEMY

"Be still, and know that I am God. I will be exalted among
the nations. I will be exalted in the earth."
— Psalm 46:10 WEB

Sovereign God, I bow before Your majesty. You silence the roaring
of the adversary and still the raging of the enemy. You command
peace where there was confusion, and You decree stillness where
there was chaos. In Your presence, the noise of my foes is drowned,
and their threats are made void.

I decree that every voice of the accuser against me is silenced now.
Every loud boast of the wicked is brought to nothing. The tumult of
the enemy cannot prevail, for You, O Lord, are exalted above the
nations, and Your throne rules over all. Let every demonic noise
that rises against my family be swallowed up in Your divine
stillness.

Father, I exalt You in my home, my workplace, my city, and my
generation. Your name is lifted high above every storm, and Your
glory overshadows the works of darkness. The enemy is stripped of
influence, their devices exposed, and their sound reduced to
silence.

I rest in Your stillness, O Lord. I will not fear, for You are God over
the nations, God over my enemies, and God over my destiny. You
alone are exalted, and every rival voice is forever muted.

In Jesus' name, Amen.

DAY 20

THE GOD OF VENGEANCE ARISES

Yahweh, you God to whom vengeance belongs, you God
to whom vengeance belongs, shine out. Rise up, you judge
of the earth. Pay back the proud what they deserve.
— Psalm 94:1-2 WEB

Righteous Judge, I call upon You to arise in Your vengeance and
execute justice on behalf of my household. You are the God who
shines forth in power, exposing the wicked and repaying them
according to their works. You are not blind to their schemes, nor
deaf to their boasts. Today I summon Your holy vengeance against
every proud adversary of my soul.

O Lord, repay the wicked who seek my downfall. Scatter the
arrogant who plot against my family. Let Your fiery judgment
descend upon every unrepentant enemy of righteousness. Where
they have lifted themselves in pride, bring them low. Where they
have exalted themselves in malice, cast them down in shame.

Father, shine out in my life with the brilliance of Your justice. Let
Your vengeance shatter generational chains, overthrow ancestral
altars, and consume every evil decree issued against me. Arise, O
Judge of the earth, and let my oppressors know that You are God
alone.

Today I stand in holy boldness, declaring that the proud shall be
humbled and the wicked shall be repaid. My portion is
preservation, but their portion is destruction. The vengeance of

God shields me, the justice of God preserves me, and the fire of God destroys my enemies.

In Jesus' name, Amen.

DAY 21

TRAMPLING THE WICKED

You shall tread down the wicked; for they shall be ashes
under the soles of your feet in the day that I make, says
Yahweh of Armies.
— Malachi 4:3 WEB

Mighty God of justice, I lift my voice in triumph today, declaring
that every wicked power assigned against my life and family is
destined to be trampled underfoot. You, Lord of Armies, have
decreed their end. You have declared that they shall be reduced to
ashes, powerless, lifeless, and unable to rise again. I stand in that
prophetic reality and proclaim that the forces of darkness that have
risen against me are already judged and overthrown.

By the authority of Christ's victory, I crush every serpent and
scorpion that has slithered into my household, my health, my
finances, and my destiny. Their time of operation is over. Father, I
decree that my feet are anointed with fire and dominion to tread
down the adversaries of my soul. No longer shall fear, torment, or
oppression rule in my dwelling, for I stand clothed in Your strength.

Every witchcraft projection, every curse uttered, every demonic
alliance, I break them down to dust and ashes. Their works are
shattered beyond repair. My family and I will no longer be
intimidated, for You have placed us in a position of triumph.

O consuming fire, arise and let the works of the wicked be burned
to nothingness. As they are reduced to ashes, let Your glory be

exalted in my life. My victory is irreversible because You have spoken it. I rejoice that the power of the enemy has no future in my story.

In Jesus' name, Amen.

DAY 22

VICTORY THROUGH CHRIST

But thanks be to God, who gives us the victory through
our Lord Jesus Christ.
— 1 Corinthians 15:57 WEB

O God of triumph, I lift up a shout of praise to You today! My heart
resounds with thanksgiving because through the blood of Jesus
Christ, the eternal Victor, I am no longer bound by defeat. The
grave could not hold Him, death could not conquer Him, and
because I am hidden in Him, I walk in unshakable victory.

Lord, I declare that every power contending with my life and
destiny is already defeated. No weapon fashioned against me shall
prosper because the cross has silenced every accuser. I refuse to
bow to fear, intimidation, or oppression. My family and I are
covered in the triumph of Christ, and we march forward knowing
the outcome has already been sealed by His resurrection power.

I cancel the assignments of darkness that seek to infiltrate my
home, my health, my calling, or my provision. By the victory of
Jesus, I strip them of their authority and break their hold. Every
plan of destruction collapses at the feet of Christ, for He reigns
supreme and has delivered victory into my hands.

Lord, let the fragrance of triumph surround me. Let songs of
victory fill my household. Where the enemy sought to bring sorrow,
I decree joy. Where he sought to cause confusion, I declare clarity

and peace. My testimony is that I always triumph through Christ. In Jesus' name, Amen.

DAY 23

Pursuing to Destroy

I struck them, so that they were not able to rise. They fell
under my feet.
— Psalm 18:38 WEB

Warrior King, I rise today in the strength of Your Spirit, declaring
that every enemy arrayed against my soul will fall and never rise
again. You, O Lord, empower my hands for battle and my feet for
conquest. The adversaries that once pursued me will stumble and
collapse under the authority of Your power working in me.

I pursue every demonic power that has sought to pursue my
destiny. I overtake them with the sword of the Spirit, and I strike
them down by the fire of the Lord. They shall not recover, they shall
not regroup, and they shall not return. The cycle of oppression is
broken. I declare final judgment against the works of witchcraft,
manipulation, and ancestral strongholds.

Father, You have placed my enemies beneath my feet. Depression,
fear, delay, and sickness—all are crushed under the weight of
Christ's victory. I declare that they have no capacity to rise again.
The altars that empowered them are dismantled, and their voices
are silenced forever.

Lord, establish me in permanent victory. Let my children walk in
the freedom of this conquest. Let my household live as a testimony
that the wicked may rise against us, but they will surely fall and

never rise again. My feet walk in triumph because of You, O God. In Jesus' name, Amen.

DAY 24

ARISE, O LORD

Arise, Yahweh! Save me, my God! For you have struck all of my enemies on the cheek bone. You have broken the teeth of the wicked.
— Psalm 3:7 WEB

O Lord my Deliverer, I cry out with holy passion—Arise! Manifest Your power over every dark power contending with my life. You are the Mighty Warrior who defends the helpless and shatters the strength of the wicked. You have promised to break their teeth, stripping them of their bite, their power, and their intimidation. Today I declare that every enemy of my destiny is disarmed and disgraced.

Father, I lift my family before You and declare that their enemies will not prevail. Every voice that has risen to devour us is silenced. Every plot against our future is broken. You, O Lord, strike them on the cheek, humiliating their pride and exposing their weakness. Their power to afflict us is cut off at the root.

I decree that the wicked will have no room to swallow up my joy or sabotage my progress. Their teeth are broken, their grip shattered, their influence destroyed. They scatter in confusion while my household rises in glory.

Lord, thank You that when You arise, the enemy is scattered. Thank You that salvation belongs to You, and Your blessing rests upon me and my family. We stand shielded under Your power, rejoicing that our enemies are crushed beyond recovery.

In Jesus' name, Amen.

DAY 25

No Enchantment Shall Stand

Surely there is no enchantment with Jacob; Neither is
there any divination with Israel. Now it shall be said of
Jacob and of Israel, What has God done!
— Numbers 23:23 WEB

Faithful God, I exalt You today as the Shield of my family and the
Defender of our inheritance. No spell, no divination, no
incantation can ever prevail against those whom You have chosen
and redeemed by the blood of the Lamb. I stand as Your child and
declare boldly that every enchantment sent against me and my
household is nullified and rendered powerless.

Lord, I decree that the voices of sorcery, witchcraft, and occult
powers shall not prosper in my life. No curse shall alight upon me
because I am covered in the covenant of blessing. Every evil
utterance spoken against my destiny returns to the sender, and
every altar erected against me crumbles to dust.

Instead of enchantments working, it shall be declared, "See what
God has done!" My life will broadcast Your wonders, my household
will testify of Your goodness, and my destiny will shine forth with
undeniable breakthroughs. The works of darkness will only amplify
the glory of my Deliverer.

Father, I cancel every demonic forecast over my future. No
divination can redirect my path. I am sealed in covenant blood, and
no sorcerer can tamper with that divine seal. Let it be proclaimed

among men and angels that my life is the evidence of God's mighty works.

In Jesus' name, Amen.

DAY 26

CRUSHED BEFORE MY FACE

Your hand will be lifted up above your adversaries, and all
of your enemies will be cut off.
—Micah 5:9 WEB

O Lord of Hosts, my Mighty Deliverer, I lift my voice today in holy
defiance against every enemy rising against me and my family. By
Your word, You have declared that my hand will be lifted high above
my adversaries, and that every enemy shall be cut off. I take hold of
this prophetic promise and declare that every demonic stronghold
seeking to control my destiny is shattered in Your power.

Let the forces of darkness that surround my household be
confounded. Let the ancient curses, generational bondages, and
satanic decrees assigned against me be broken by the fire of Your
Spirit. I decree that the enemies of my progress, health, and
inheritance shall be cut off without remedy. They will fall by their
own devices and collapse under the weight of their rebellion against
the Lord Most High.

Father, let my hand be exalted over poverty, sickness, confusion,
and fear. Lift me above every evil altar that has been raised against
me. I stand tall, not by my might, but by Your Spirit. I refuse to bow
to intimidation, manipulation, or opposition from the kingdom of
darkness.

O God, arise and vindicate Your covenant in my life. Let every
enemy of my peace be crushed. Let the adversaries of my children

and household be scattered. Today, I walk in the victory of Christ and wield divine authority to destroy the works of darkness. My enemies are cut off, and my inheritance is secure in You.

In Jesus' name, Amen.

DAY 27

The Wicked Stumble and Fall

When evildoers came at me to eat up my flesh, even my
adversaries and my foes, they stumbled and fell.
—Psalm 27:2 WEB

Mighty Warrior and Shield of my life, I exalt You as my defender
and my strength. You have declared that when the wicked rise
against me, they shall stumble and fall. I declare this over my life
and my family: every adversary that seeks to devour us shall
collapse before the consuming fire of God.

Every satanic agent, every demonic plot, every evil spirit sent to
devour our health, our joy, and our progress—I command them to
stumble. Let the darkness lose its footing; let the pursuers of my
soul fall into their own traps. Let the devourer be silenced, and let
the destroyer be cast down.

Father, cause the enemies who hunt for my peace to lose their
strength. Let their voices be silenced in confusion. Every
conspiracy of witches, warlocks, or hidden oppressors shall
backfire. Their arrows shall return to their own hearts, and their
plans shall disintegrate into nothingness.

I declare over my household that we will not be meat for the enemy.
We are covered in the blood of Jesus and shielded by the Lord of
Hosts. My adversaries may rise, but they will stumble. They may
gather, but they will fall. Victory is mine through the unfailing
Word of God. In Jesus' name, Amen.

DAY 28

Overcoming by the Blood

They overcame him because of the Lamb's blood, and
because of the word of their testimony. They didn't love
their life, even to death.
—Revelation 12:11 WEB

Eternal Redeemer, I lift my voice in triumph today. By the blood of
the Lamb, I stand in victory over the accuser of my soul. The blood
speaks louder than the voice of condemnation, louder than curses,
louder than the lies of the enemy. I declare that my household and
I are overcomers by this eternal blood.

By the word of my testimony, I decree that the adversary is silenced.
I testify that Jesus Christ has redeemed me, justified me, and seated
me with Him in heavenly places. No accusation can stand against
me; no curse can hold me; no bondage can prevail. I nullify every
satanic word spoken over my life and over my family. Let those
words be broken, scattered, and destroyed forever.

Father, I choose courage over fear, faith over despair, and truth over
deception. The enemy may seek to intimidate, but I will not bow.
By the blood, I cancel evil works—witchcraft, sorcery, sickness, and
strife. They are nullified at the cross. I trample upon the serpent and
the scorpion in the authority of Christ's blood.

Today I stand clothed in the power of the Lamb. My testimony is
sure, my covering is unbreakable, and my victory is eternal. Every

adversary is overcome, every stronghold is broken, and every yoke is destroyed.

In Jesus' name, Amen.

DAY 29

LET GOD ARISE

Let God arise! Let his enemies be scattered! Let them who
hate him also flee before him.
—Psalm 68:1 WEB

Ancient of Days, Mighty God, I call upon You to arise in Your
power. Let every enemy surrounding my life and family be
scattered. Let those who hate You and plot against Your children
flee in terror before Your holy presence.

Lord, rise up against the strongholds of darkness working in secret.
Rise up against the adversaries who scheme against my health, my
children, and my future. Scatter every demonic confederacy, every
satanic council, and every evil network that conspires to hinder me.
Let the consuming fire of Your presence drive them into desolation.

I decree by Your Word that no weapon formed against me shall
prosper. Let those who dig pits for me fall into them. Let the
destroyer be destroyed. Let the hunter become the hunted, and let
the oppressor be swallowed in his own traps. Father, arise as my
Defender and scatter the enemy beyond recovery.

Lord, as You arise in my life, let peace, restoration, and blessing
flow. Let joy replace sorrow, and let triumph overthrow defeat. My
enemies are scattered, their devices destroyed, their works cut off
forever.

In Jesus' name, Amen.

DAY 30

TEARING DOWN STRONGHOLDS

"Behold, I have today set you over the nations and over the kingdoms, to root out and to tear down, to destroy and to overthrow, to build and to plant."
—Jeremiah 1:10 WEB

Lord God Almighty, You have set me as a warrior with authority in Christ. By Your Word, I have been empowered to root out, to pull down, to destroy, and to overthrow every work of darkness. Today I rise in that authority, standing firm in Your covenant, to destroy the strongholds of the enemy in my life and my family.

I root out every seed of fear, despair, and confusion planted by the enemy. I tear down every demonic altar, every satanic throne, and every high place lifted against Your will. Let the power of witchcraft and sorcery be utterly demolished. I overthrow every evil decree and every curse spoken against my lineage.

Father, I destroy the works of sickness, oppression, and barrenness. Let every evil power that has stood over my household be cast down. I release divine judgment upon principalities and powers that resist Your plan. No kingdom of darkness will prevail over the kingdom of Christ within me.

Now, O Lord, I declare the season of building and planting. Plant Your peace in my home. Build up my destiny in righteousness. Establish my children in strength and joy. Let newness of life spring forth as the ruins of the enemy's works are swept away. In Jesus' name, Amen.

EPILOGUE

You have prayed. You have declared. You have wielded the sword of the Spirit, and you have broken down strongholds by the authority of God's Word. But the journey does not end here—this is only the beginning.

Spiritual warfare is not a one-time event; it is a lifestyle of vigilance, prayer, and victory. The enemy does not rest, but neither does the power of God within you. What comes next is a life lived in continual awareness of your authority in Christ. Every day, you must rise as a warrior, clothed in the armor of God, refusing to yield ground to darkness.

Keep your spiritual weapons sharp. Continue to declare God's Word over your life and family. Refuse to allow fear, doubt, or compromise to creep back into the spaces you have reclaimed. Build on the ruins of the enemy's works by planting the promises of God—speaking life, walking in holiness, and cultivating a heart of worship.

Now that you have destroyed strongholds, it is time to establish strong foundations. Guard your household with prayer. Speak blessings over your children and future generations. Live in the daily awareness that you are seated with Christ in heavenly places, far above principalities and powers. Let every day become an opportunity to enforce His victory in new areas of your life.

The enemy is defeated, but you are called to enforce that defeat. Keep declaring. Keep resisting. Keep standing. As you do, the victory of Christ will not only protect you but also shine through you—bringing light to those still trapped in darkness.

The battle is not over, but neither is your authority. Step forward with boldness, and live as one who destroys the works of the enemy by the unstoppable power of God.

Encourage Others with Your Story

If this prayer guide has strengthened your faith, deepened your intercession, or helped you stand in the gap, would you consider leaving a short review on Amazon? Your feedback not only encourages others but also helps more believers discover this resource and join in the prayer movement. Every review—just a few sentences—makes a difference. Thank you for being part of this movement.

MORE FROM PRAYERSCRIPTS

COMMAND YOUR DESTINY SERIES

Command Your Morning:

30 Days of Prayers and Declarations to Seize Your Day and Shape Your Destiny

There is a battle over every morning—and every believer must choose to either drift into the day or command it.

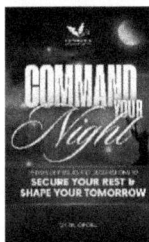

Command Your Night:

30 Days of Prayers and Declarations to Secure Your Rest and Shape Your Tomorrow

Every night is a spiritual battlefield—what you do before you sleep can determine the course of your tomorrow.

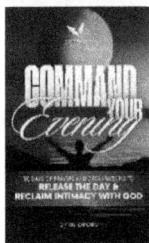

Command Your Evening:

30 Days of Prayers and Declarations to Release the Day and Reclaim Intimacy with God

There is a battle over every transition—and evening is one of the most spiritually neglected.

EXPOSING THE ENEMY SERIES

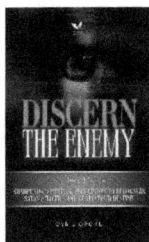

Discern the Enemy:

Sharpening Spiritual Perception to Recognize Satan's Tactics and Guard Your Destiny

The greatest danger is not the enemy you can see—it is the one you cannot. Can you recognize the enemy before he strikes?

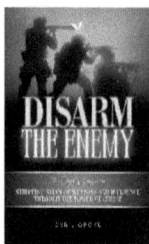

Disarm the Enemy:

Stripping Satan of Weapons and Influence Through the Power of Christ

Are you tired of feeling like the enemy has the upper hand in your life? It's time to take back your ground, silence the lies of darkness, and walk in the unstoppable authority of Christ.

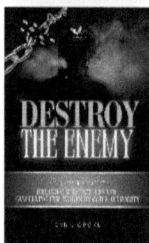

Destroy the Enemy:

Breaking Strongholds and Cancelling Evil Works by God's Authority

Are you tired of living under the weight of unseen battles? It's time to rise up and destroy the enemy's works in your life.

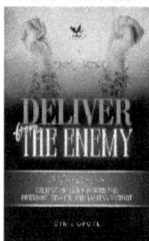

Deliver from the Enemy:

Calling on God's Power for Freedom, Rescue, and Lasting Victory

Break free from spiritual attacks and experience God's mighty deliverance in every battle.

Declare Against the Enemy:

Speaking God's Word Boldly to Enforce Triumph Over Darkness

What if you could silence the enemy's schemes, protect your family, and walk boldly into every God-ordained assignment with unshakable authority?

SPIRITUAL WARFARE SERIES

Scriptures & Prayers for Deliverance from Trouble:

40 Days of Prayer for When Life Feels Overwhelming

Are you walking through a season where life feels heavy and your prayers feel weak?

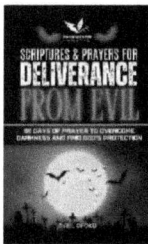

Scriptures & Prayers for Deliverance from Evil:

50 Days of Prayer to Overcome Darkness and Find God's Protection

When darkness presses in, how do you pray?

Scriptures & Prayers for Engaging the Enemy:

70 Days of Prayer to Rebuke the Enemy and Release God's Power

You weren't called to run from the battle—you were anointed to win it.

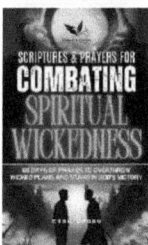

Scriptures & Prayers for Combating Spiritual Wickedness:

50 Days of Prayer to Overthrow Wicked Plans and Stand in God's Victory

Are you facing opposition that feels deeper than the natural? You're not imagining it—and you're not powerless.

THE BLOOD COVENANT SERIES

Pardon Through the Blood:

60 Days of Prayers for Total Forgiveness and Freedom

Guilt is a prison. The blood of Jesus holds the key.

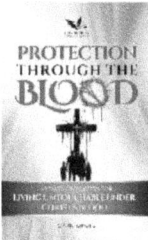

Protection Through the Blood:

60 Days of Prayers for Living Untouchable Under Christ's Blood

You are not helpless. You are not exposed. You are covered—completely—by the blood of Jesus.

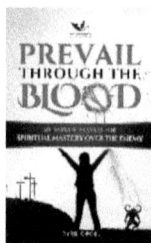

Prevail Through the Blood:

60 Days of Prayers for Spiritual Mastery Over the Enemy

What if every scheme of the enemy against your life could be dismantled—by one unstoppable weapon?

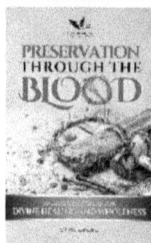

Preservation Through the Blood:

60 Days of Prayers for Divine Healing and Wholeness

Unlock Lasting Healing and Wholeness Through the Blood of Jesus

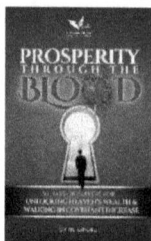

Prosperity Through the Blood:

60 Days of Prayers for Unlocking Heaven's Wealth and Walking in Covenant Increase

You were redeemed for more than survival—you were redeemed to prosper.

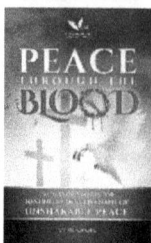

Peace Through the Blood:

60 Days of Prayers for Resting in the Covenant of Unshakable Peace

Are you ready to silence every storm of the mind, heart, and home—once and for all?

Standing in the Gap for Covenant Awakening:

30 Days of Prayer for National Repentance, Righteous Leadership & God's Sovereign Rule

What if your prayers could help turn the tide of a nation?

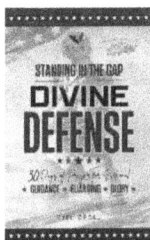

Standing in the Gap for Divine Defense:

30 Days of Prayer for National Guidance, Guarding & Glory

When the foundations of a nation feel as if they're shaking, prayer is the strongest fortress you can build.

Standing in the Gap for National Healing:

40 Days of Prayer for Reconciliation, Righteousness, and Restoration

What if your prayers could help heal a nation? What if God is waiting for someone—like you—to stand in the gap?

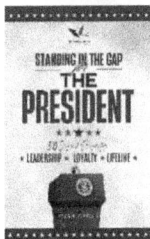

Standing in the Gap for The President:

50 Days of Prayer for Leadership, Loyalty, and Lifeline

When a nation's leader is under spiritual siege, will you answer the call to stand in the gap?

www.ingramcontent.com/pod-product-compliance
Lightning Source LLC
Chambersburg PA
CBHW060159070426

42447CB00033B/2233